C0UNT1NG TH3 DAY$

A 31-day devotional for accountants, bookkeepers, and financial folk

By an accountant
Leeann Betts

C0UNT1NG TH3 DAY$

Copyright

All Scripture quotations, unless otherwise indicated, are taken from the Holy Bible, New International Version®, NIV®. Copyright ©1973, 1978, 1984, 2011 by Biblica, Inc.™ Used by permission of Zondervan. All rights reserved worldwide. www.zondervan.com The "NIV" and "New International Version" are trademarks registered in the United States Patent and Trademark Office by Biblica, Inc.™

Copyright © 2015 Leeann Betts

All rights reserved.

ISBN-13: 978-1-943688-13-5

Published by PLS Bookworks, Denver, CO

Where Publishing Dreams Become Reality

Other Books Available from

Donna Schlachter and Leeann Betts

Donna Schlachter:
Second Chances and Second Cups
A sweet collection of stories of second chances from a second-chance God.

Leeann Betts:
No Accounting for Murder: Book 1 in By the Numbers series
Follow Carly Turnquist, forensic accountant, as she pokes her nose in to
one mystery after the other.
There Was A Crooked Man: Book 2 in By the Numbers series --
follow Carly as a working vacation turns into a nightmare when she joins husband Mike in New Mexico and bodies start turning up
Unbalanced : Book 3 in By the Numbers series (January 2016)
Five and Twenty Blackbirds : Book 4 in By the Numbers series (April 2016)

By Donna and Leeann:
Nuggets of Writing Gold-- a compilation of essays and articles on the craft of writing.

All books available at Amazon.com (digital and print) and Smashwords.com (digital only)

Follow us at:
Donna: www.HiStoryThruTheAges.wordpress.com
www.HiStoryThruTheAges.com
Leeann: www.AllBettsAreOff.wordpress.com
www.LeeannBetts.com

We are also active on Facebook and Twitter

Foreword

This book was born of an idea that started as a seed that soon bloomed into a project. My goal in writing this book was to provide a tool for accountants and other financial folk, who often work day after day in the cut-throat world of big business.

My prayer is that as you work your way through these daily devotions, that you will use them as a jumping-off point for your daily quiet time with the Lord. Please use the space provided to journal and record your time with God, and ask Him to reveal something special to you today.

Each one will take you five minutes or less, perfect for quieting your heart at the beginning of a hectic day, or ideal for taking a breather in the middle of a day gone wrong. You could even use them during prayer time at the end of the day, as you plan the next day and commit your time to the Lord.

Whenever you choose to sit for a few minutes, offer that time to God, ask Him to show you what He has planned for you, and let Him lead you where He wants you to go.

All glory and honor and power and praise be to Him.

Day 1

Bean Counter

Genesis 1:22 God blessed them and said, "Be fruitful and increase in number and fill the water in the seas, and let the birds increase on the earth." (NIV)

Bean counter.

I'd heard it a hundred times, and it wasn't any more funny this time than the first time.

Bean counter.

Made what I did sound inane and unimportant. A make-work project.

But that wasn't true. God didn't create me to be a bean counter. He created me with an orderly and systematic mind that quickly and easily grasped the abstract concept of numbers and their relationship to each other. Not everyone has that gift. And unless I view it as a gift, I could easily get discouraged by others' perception of my abilities.

I love numbers, and I appreciate them. I love the fact that everything else may change, but numbers never do. Kind of like God. The same today, yesterday, and forever. God has an appreciation for numbers, too. When He blessed the animals and birds, and told them to increase in number, He was witnessing the first addition and multiplication operations.

When I consider that mathematics and numbers were one of the first things done on this earth, that makes my job much more important, somehow.

God, never let me consider the gift You have given me to be substandard to someone else's, just because it may seem boring to them. Remind me that You made me this way because I am made in Your image, and You love numbers. Amen.

C0UNT1NG TH3 DAY$

My Journal

Day 2
Days Without Number

Jeremiah 2:32 Does a maiden forget her jewelry, a bride her wedding ornaments? Yet my people have forgotten me, days without number. (NIV)

At the bank where I worked, we had the old-fashioned kind of adding machines, the large contraption with the punch numbers, similar to an old cash register. When the power went out, we could still do some work using a pull handle to work the machine.

One day, I needed to move this old adding machine. I reached over to pull the plug from the wall, and got a huge shock. I fell on the floor, and the plug sizzled and smoked while I tried to regain my bearings and my senses.

Apparently, this machine's days were numbered.

And mine were almost.

Thankfully, I had many more days, which I've sought to enjoy in service to my Lord. I don't want to know how many days I have left, to be honest. To me, my days are without number. That doesn't mean I expect to live forever, except in a spiritual sense. But, not knowing the date I will die gives me a sense of unnumbered days.

C0UNT1NG TH3 DAY$

Today, as we meditate on our scripture verse, ask the Lord to show you how He adorns you with ornaments, how beautiful you are to Him. Ask Him to dance over you with joy, and sing over You with rejoicing.

Lord God, I thank You and praise You for each and every one of my days. I know they are a gift from You, and I choose to cherish this one. In Jesus' name, Amen.

C0UNT1NG TH3 DAY$

My Journal

Day 3
Multiply the Blessings

Mark 6:41 Taking the five loaves and the two fish and looking up to heaven, He gave thanks and broke the loaves. Then He gave them to His disciples to set before the people. He also divided the two fish among them all. (NIV)

As financial folk, we can agree that multiplication and division are simply functions of addition; shorthand, as it were, for mathematics. And usually we don't see both functions in the same equation.

However, in this verse, we see Jesus multiplying and dividing, and still coming up with a number greater than the number He started with. He took five loaves and two fishes and gave thanks. In the original language, the word for "blessed" is used. Blessing implies increase, multiplication.

Then He broke the loaves and the fish and divided the food amongst the people. In this instance, there were five thousand men present, not including women and children.

Now that's the kind of multiplication and division I'm sure some of our clients would like to see!

Today, as you consider how God takes your small talents and little bit of time and multiplies and divides them for His purposes, remember that God doesn't call the qualified; He qualifies the called.

C0UNT1NG TH3 DAY$

He will make up the difference between what you know and what He needs, between your energy and His projects, and between your abilities and His good plans for you.

God Almighty, I praise You for all You have done in my life, and for the ways You are using me to make an eternal difference for Your kingdom. In Jesus' name, Amen.

C0UNT1NG TH3 DAY$

My Journal

Day 4

How Long is a Lifetime?

Psalm 39:4 Show me, O LORD, my life's end and the number of my days; let me know how fleeting is my life.(NIV)

I remember when I was hired for my first "real" job. Not an after-school job or a between-semesters job, but a full-time job. The bank had me fill out some paperwork, and one of them was for my retirement plan. I was all of eighteen years old, and retirement was far from my mind. I'll never forget the date on the form when I could start to draw on my pension, if I stayed with the bank long enough: 2013. My fifty-fifth birthday.

As I stared at that number—2013—which was thirty-five years in the future, I thought, "I'll never live that long". Not that I thought I would die young, but it's just when you're 18, 55 seems OLD.

Well, I did make it to 55, and beyond. I didn't stay with the bank. I moved on after about six years. And I'm glad that God chose to number my days beyond my retirement date.

Because life is fleeting. As I look back to those days when I signed that paperwork, it seems like just a few years have passed. Yet my knees tell me different.

C0UNT1NG TH3 DAY$

God has numbered all of our days. He's numbered the hairs on our head, has counted and named the stars in the sky, and still He's involved in our lives at a deeply personal level.

Today, remember that for every star you see in the sky, God who knows its name. And that same God knows your name.

Dear Father, thank You for knowing me by name. Thank You for taking such good care of me that You know the number of hairs on my head and the number of days You've given me. Remind me to be thankful for each. In Jesus' name, Amen.

C0UNT1NG TH3 DAY$

My Journal

Day 5
Distractions

Deuteronomy 8:18 But remember the LORD your God, for it is He who gives you the ability to produce wealth, and so confirms His covenant, which He swore to your forefathers, as it is today. (NIV)

I was using a calculator to add up a long list of numbers one day, and the phone rang. I looked up to check the caller ID, and got distracted. Since I wasn't using a machine tape (that's a lesson for another day), I didn't know where I'd left off.

I had to start all over again.

Our walk with the Lord can seem like that sometimes. One step forward, two back. But we forget the rest of the verse—it is He who gives you the ability. We aren't called to serve the Lord because we're qualified. We are qualified because He calls us. He continues to work in us every day. There is no arriving in the Christian life.

So, the next time you think you can't possibly learn any more about God, remember this: He confirms His covenant, and one of His promises is that He who began a good work in you, will be faithful to complete it.

That means that no amount of doing on your part will get you to where you're going.

That's God's job.

C0UNT1NG TH3 DAY$

Father in Heaven, thank You for reminding me that I belong to You, not only my physical body and my soul, but also the work of my hands and the praises of my tongue. May everything I do today glorify You. In Jesus' name, Amen.

C0UNT1NG TH3 DAY$

My Journal

Day 6
Worthy of the Kingdom

II Thessalonians 1:5 All this is evidence that God's judgment is right, and as a result you will be counted worthy of the kingdom of God, for which you are suffering. (NIV)

Creating financial statements for a company is simply a matter of putting things in the correct categories and adding up the numbers properly. Note I used those two adjectives "correct" and "properly". Because the truth is, if you do either of those actions improperly or incorrectly, you might just as well have not done the work at all.

Errors in categorization and addition result in revised tax returns, corrected audited statements, loss of credibility, and perhaps even criminal charges. We don't want that for our clients or for ourselves.

In the same way, if God doesn't count us worthy of His kingdom, we can face some unpleasant outcomes, including temporary separation from Him because of our sin, eternal separation because of our unrepentance, momentary separation because of our disobedience, and broken relationships with loved ones because of our unforgiveness.

But because we know God's judgment is right, correct, and just, we can trust that He knows the motives of our hearts and ascribes to us His righteousness to make up the difference. We can never be good enough to get into heaven on our own, and we can never be bad enough not to get into heaven through Jesus.

Today, as you focus on God's righteousness, thank Him for sending His Son Jesus to be your righteousness.

God, thank you for sending Your Son to die for me. Thank You for making me right with You. In Jesus' name, Amen.

C0UNT1NG TH3 DAY$

My Journal

Day 7
Staying Balanced

Matthew 10:30 And even the very hairs of your head are all numbered. (NIV)

    I had a friend one time who hated to balance her check book. One day, she shoved the offending little register at me and said, "Here, see if you can figure out why I'm overdrawn when I should have $300."

    I scanned her register and noted she had several entries of varying amounts for ESP. Thinking this was perhaps an online purchase she was making on a regular basis, I asked her about it.

    She grinned at me, kind of sheepishly, and said, "No, that's where I balanced my checkbook to my bank balance. ESP stands for Error Some Place."

    Right away I could see her problem. She was trying to balance her account to a moving target without taking into consideration uncleared checks and deposits.

    Knowing the number of hairs on your head would also be a kind of moving target. Hairs fall out, hairs grow in. Hairs break off. Is that a full hair or a half hair? Sounds ridiculous, doesn't it?

    And yet God tells us He is concerned enough about the

seeming trivialities of our lives that He knows the number of hairs on our head. He is detailed enough to keep track of such an inconsequential fact.

And it's not the number that's important. It's the idea that He cares enough to know.

As you meditate on that today, remember that the God who knows the smallest detail about you has chosen to cast your sin as far as the east is from the west, never to be remembered again.

Lord God Almighty, I bask in the knowledge of Your great love for me. Help me to remember this when everything around me crowds in and tries to crowd You out. In Jesus' name, Amen.

C0UNT1NG TH3 DAY$

My Journal

Day 8

Inventory Control

Psalm 48:12 Walk about Zion, go around her, count her towers, (NIV)

I used to work in a grocery store before we had computers and inventory control systems. Everything was done manually, including giving change, weighing produce, and balancing at the end of the shift.

Inventory was done by hauling a step stool up and down the aisles, counting every product on the shelves by type, rotating the stock if needed, and moving misplaced cans and boxes to their proper locations.

You can imagine that counting all the bottles and containers and items in a grocery store could become confusing, particularly as so many products look the same.

I'm sure once computerized inventory control came into place, the stock-taker's job became much simpler, although a physical inventory where each item was counted still has to be done at least on an annual basis.

What a joy to know that God, the ultimate expert in inventory control—after all, He knows the number of hairs on your head, the number of your days, every star by name, every sparrow that falls—has your concerns and needs at the top of His list. We don't need to wait a year for Him to realize a prayer was misplaced or a gift was misaddressed.

Today, as you meditate on our scripture verse, consider how our infinite God can keep track of our finite needs, and thank Him for His attention to detail.

Heavenly Father, thank You for setting the example for me, for reminding me that I am important to You. Thank You for giving me a place in Your kingdom. In Jesus' name, Amen.

C0UNT1NG TH3 DAY$

My Journal

Day 9
Growing in Faith

Acts 16:5 So the churches were strengthened in the faith and grew daily in numbers. (NIV)

I once had a client whose sole purpose was to make money. To accomplish this, he treated his employees harshly, expecting them to put in the same kind of crazy hours he did. He cheated his suppliers, and he harassed his clients to pay their bills early, even though he was always late paying his own bills.

In short, he was downright mean.

And in the end, it didn't matter how much money he made. He always wanted more.

In our verse today, we see that God doesn't put the emphasis on numbers. He stresses that growing in our faith is the goal, and the blessing comes as a result of that growth. Jesus said, "What does it prosper a man if he gains the whole world and loses his soul?" My paraphrase: all the money in the world won't buy your way into heaven.

So how do we grow in faith? Through spending time with God in prayer and reading His word. Through regular church attendance where we hear the Word of God preached, so we can exercise our gifts in a safe place, and to receive encouragement, and are able to encourage, a body of like-minded believers.

And as we grow in our faith, God will give the increase. You've got His word on it.

Heavenly God, Who reached down from heaven and touched my heart, Who chose me from before the beginning of time, please touch me now and give me a hunger for You. In Jesus' name, Amen.

C0UNT1NG TH3 DAY$

My Journal

Day 10
Few in Number

Genesis 34:30 Then Jacob said to Simeon and Levi, "You have brought trouble on me by making me a stench to the Canaanites and Perizzites, the people living in this land. We are few in number, and if they join forces against me and attack me, I and my household will be destroyed." (NIV)

Few in number. When we're talking overdraft, that's a good thing. When we're talking money for payroll, that's another problem entirely. At one point, I worked for a company that was constantly running up against its overdraft limit. Things got so bad, we weren't able to pay our bills. Vendors would call, and I would have the receptionist take messages because I couldn't deal with talking to these people every day.

And while they were calling on one line, I was calling our clients on another, trying to get them to pay us on time so we could pay our vendors. Sometimes our suppliers had to wait 90 or 120 because our clients were slow paying us.

The solution? For us it was to get an increase in our overdraft limit. How did that work out? Well, we increased our debt, paid off some suppliers who were threatening legal action, and gained some breathing room. But the respite was false. Because pretty soon we were back in the same position of having to delay payment of suppliers.

The final solution? We had to get more strict with our own expenses, cutting back where we were able. Which meant we let some staff go, cut hours for others, didn't have a Christmas bonus for a couple of years. We also had to get more strict with our clients, explaining to them that if they wanted their work done on time, we expected payment on time. A couple of threatened delays to their projects brought their payments more current.

Sometimes it can seem that the enemy is ganging up on us, intent on destroying us. The truth is, he needs only to distract us from the work of the Lord in order to gain an upper hand in our lives. Just as our lack of funds was a distraction to us, perceived lack in our lives can distract us from praising God for what He has already done for us.

Today, focus on what God has already done for you. Give thanks with a grateful heart.

Lord God, forgive me for my selfishness in the past. Thank You for reminding me that while we are under Your protection, the enemy isn't able to touch us. Keep me focused on Your will for my life. In Jesus' name. Amen.

C0UNT1NG TH3 DAY$

My Journal

Day 11
Business Matters

John 15:15 I no longer call you servants, because a servant does not know his master's business. Instead, I have called you friends, for everything that I learned from my Father I have made known to you. (NIV)

Studies show that the number one thing that causes businesses to fail is lack of capital. People start a business and don't have enough money set aside to live on until the company starts showing a profit. Often that's because they didn't have a strong business plan to begin with. Or they over-estimated their product or service. Or they underestimated the length of time required to get the product from the idea stage into the customer's hands.

In other words, they didn't truly know their business.

In our scripture today, we see that servants (read: employees) don't know their master's business. Employees are there typically to do a job and get paid a wage. It's a contract that's made, either formally or informally, between the employer and the worker.

I have seen instances where employees showed such indifference to the business that they ran it into the ground by slowing productivity and increasing labor costs. When this happens, it becomes obvious very quickly that the employee doesn't know the business, since the owner's goal is to make a profit.

Do we treat God this way? Is He simply a Sugar-Daddy, waiting to hand over whatever we want? Can we take, take, take, and never give back? You might wonder what we could possibly give the Creator of the Universe? What do we have that He wants?

Our praise. God has said that if we don't praise Him, He'll have the rocks cry out. Why does He need our praise? As our ultimate demonstration of our love for Him. He is magnified and glorified when we praise Him.

Today, as we meditate on this scripture, let's consider how many ways we can show God how much we love Him.

Lover of my soul, You are worthy of all I can say, all I can do. You are the creator of every breath I take, and I worship You with all that I am. Amen.

C0UNT1NG TH3 DAY$

My Journal

Day 12
Faithful Numbers

Psalm 90:12 Teach us to number our days aright, that we may gain a heart of wisdom.(NIV)

I love numbers. They are faithful and true. They don't change. They don't lie. They are what they are. For me, numbers are an abstract indicator of a world that isn't so abstract sometimes. Emotions can't be enumerated. Feelings can't be counted. Even figuring out how many words we speak or miles we walk each day can be overwhelming. And no matter how big the number, you can always add one more and get a bigger number.

This love of numbers might seem ordinary to you. After all, I'm talking to accountants, bookkeepers, financial people who eat, sleep, and dream numbers. But I struggled with numbers when I was in early grades in school.

I remember drying dishes after supper when I was about seven, and my mother trying to run through my times tables with me. I was fine up to the five-times, but after that, everything got fuzzy.

And then one day my father showed me a pattern. How I could add the numbers together in my head real quick when I got to things like the seven times, eight times, and nine times tables.

And suddenly even the confusing pattern of multiplication made sense. It was addition in shorthand! From there I learned long multiplication and complicated division. All variations on addition.

In the same way, growing in Christ is a matter of building on one lesson learned at a time. God doesn't expect us to know everything at once. He does expect us to grow and change into His likeness and image over time.

And just as multiplication is a variation on addition, growing in Christ is a variation of the love we have for Him. Because we love Him, we want to be like him.

Today, as you meditate on this idea, remember that God multiplies Himself in us and through us.

Heavenly Father, thank You for wanting to be in my life, and thank You for taking time to grow me into what You know I can be. In Jesus' name, Amen.

C0UNT1NG TH3 DAY$

My Journal

Day 13
In Control

Exodus 5:19 The Israelite foremen realized they were in trouble when they were told, "You are not to reduce the number of bricks required of you for each day."   (NIV)

Quotas. It seems as though everywhere we turn, we're faced with quotas. Oh, they might not be called that. Sometimes they are disguised as productivity, deadlines, critical deadlines, drop-dead deadlines. But you know they are out there, hanging over your head, waiting to be done.

Quotas in and of themselves are not bad, but sometimes the expectations that go along with them can be unreasonable. Excelling at your job is a good thing, and even tying compensation to output can be good.

Until you are not in control of the circumstances.

This happened to me once in a job I had where I was paid per entry rather than by the hour. During the learning curve, my output was less so my hourly rate worked out to be less. Once I learned the job, however, my hourly rate went up as my output increased. I found quicker ways to do the work, created shortcuts that enabled me to do more in less time.

So how does this all help us in our walk of faith today and

every day? We know that God's gift of salvation is a free gift, but that doesn't mean we get to sit back and do nothing. Once we receive that gift, then the training begins. But the one thing we can depend on is that whatever God calls us to do, He also equips us. Unlike the Egyptian overlords, He will never expect us to accomplish His work without also providing the resources.

Today, as you think about this scripture verse, consider all the ways God has equipped you for the work He calls you to do.

Heavenly Father, thank You for giving me everything I need to do what You have set before me. Thank you for all the gifts and talents You have provided. Remind me to be thankful every day. In Jesus' name, Amen.

C0UNT1NG TH3 DAY$

My Journal

Day 14
Honor in Numbers

Jeremiah 30:19 From them will come songs of thanksgiving and the sound of rejoicing. I will add to their numbers, and they will not be decreased; I will bring them honor, and they will not be disdained. (NIV)

I once did bookkeeping for a small business that carried an inventory of decals. Hundreds of different kinds of decals. Each one had its own unique number, and this was in the years before bar codes and scanners.

Each time the owner sold decals, he often grouped together like kinds of decals, so, for example, if he sold one each of ten kinds of bicycle decals, and one each of ten kinds of motorcycle decals, and one each of ten kinds of dog decals, he'd put on his invoice that he sold ten bicycle, ten motorcycle, and ten dog decals.

Which might have been fine for the buyer, but this didn't work for the accountant.

Many times he ran out of decals because we had no way of knowing which were the popular sellers. And when he did inventory, his numbers always had to be adjusted.

Sometimes we had to add to his numbers, and sometimes we

had to subtract from his numbers.

Which might be okay except that not all the decals cost the same. Within the dog line, for example, some decals were a few cents more expensive because of gold trim or a slightly larger size.

There were never any songs of thanksgiving or sounds of rejoicing when we tried to reconcile his inventory with his books.

God wants us to be thankful, to rejoice in our relationship with Him. He promises to increase us, not only our wealth, but also our blessings, our health, our gifts and calling. His goal is to show His might and power through us in a fallen world.

Today, as you think of new ways to give thanks, remember that when God honors us, nobody can say anything negative about us.

Heavenly Father, thank You for wanting to show Yourself through me. I am not worthy of such honor, but You make me worthy through Your Son. Amen.

C0UNT1NG TII3 DAY$

My Journal

Day 15
Petty Cash

II Kings 12:10 Whenever they saw that there was a large amount of money in the chest, the royal secretary and the high priest came, counted the money that had been brought into the temple of the LORD, and put it into bags. (NIV)

Many businesses hold an amount of petty cash in a cash box or in a safe on their premises. This money can be used for incidental expenses such as coffee for the break room, or sometimes for something more substantial such as throwing a party.

When I worked for a law firm, we held petty cash of several hundred dollars, often replenishing that fund two or three times a week. Sometimes a delivery came in that was COD and we didn't have an account set up with that particular company. Many times documents had to be filed at the courthouse and a check hadn't been requisitioned in time. Other times we ran out of a particular office supply and couldn't wait for our order to come in.

In our scripture, the amount of money in these chests wasn't petty cash by any means. This was money being collected for a specific purpose: to rebuild the temple. Picture a chest big enough to put a person inside, like an old-fashioned pirate's chest, and you'll get an idea of how big this chest was. People gave money, gold, silver, jewels, precious metals, into this offering. And then the chest was emptied. And not once. Not twice, but whenever they saw the chest was full, they counted it and stored it away.

That's a lot of money.

And God owns all of it.

So the next time you wonder if He can answer a particular prayer, remember this chest of offerings that was emptied over and over again.

And never wonder again if He can answer.

Lord of heaven, You are a God who gives and gives. You gave Your Son, You gave us this world, the number of our days, every heartbeat and every breath. Thank you. In Jesus' name, Amen.

C0UNT1NG TH3 DAY$

My Journal

Day 16
Day Labor

Deuteronomy 24:15 Pay him his wages each day before sunset, because he is poor and is counting on it. Otherwise he may cry to the LORD against you, and you will be guilty of sin. (NIV)

The heyday of day labor offices seems to be on the decrease. The days when lines of shabbily-dressed men lined around a building waiting for someone to hire them for the day is just about over.

Today's temporary labor services have specialized, so employers can register with a bureau specific to their industry: construction, hotel, accounting, secretarial, paramedical. This is a good thing: now employers know they will get temporary help with experience in their particular field.

Receiving wages on a daily basis can be a good thing. Some folks living in day-to-day housing need money to pay for their lodging that night. No more waiting for a week or two for that first paycheck.

Even temporary work can help fill in a budget gap or assist someone who is traveling through the area who doesn't want the hassle of longer-term employment.

And while God doesn't look at us as though we were day laborers, He understands we have needs that need to be met. His word promises His children don't go hungry or need to beg. He promises us life and that more abundantly. He calls us heirs to His kingdom.

So let us focus today on the blessings of God, all that He has done for us, and all that He has given us.

God, You are indeed a most generous God, who gives all that You have to your children. Remind me, Lord, that in You there is no lack and want. In Jesus' name, Amen.

C0UNT1NG TH3 DAY$

My Journal

Day 17
Star Namer

Psalm 147:4 He determines the number of the stars and calls them each by name. (NIV)

When I'm working late in my office and I look out into the night sky, I am reminded that the God I serve knows how many stars He created, and He has named each one of them. In the book of Job, God names some of the constellations and asks Job if he knows how they came into being.

God describes himself as breathing the stars into existence.

Imagine that, we serve a star-breathing God.

And this God we serve and love breathed not only the Milky Way into being, but also hundreds of millions of other galaxies and stars, planets and constellations.

Why would He do that?

Because He could.

I don't know any other reason. For our enjoyment. So we could learn to steer our ships across the oceans by them. So we could marvel at pictures coming from manned spaceships and unmanned explorer robots deep in space.

So we could look into the night sky and wonder at a God who could be so far away, yet be so immensely intimate and personal with each one of His creation.

Today, remember that the same God who created the tiniest pin prick of light in the sky also created you, and marvel at this star-breathing God we serve.

God of wonders, You are beyond what I can comprehend, yet you are personal and intimate. Star-breather, Sin-forgiver, Immanuel, God with us. Amen.

C0UNT1NG TH3 DAY$

My Journal

Day 18

Miracle Worker

Job 5:9 He performs wonders that cannot be fathomed, miracles that cannot be counted. (NIV)

I started a new job on the first Monday in September with an advertising agency, and I neglected to ask one important question prior to accepting that position: when is your fiscal year end?

Had I asked that question, I may not have taken the job.

Their fiscal year end was the end of September.

And they'd not had a full-time accountant since May of that year, at which point the woman was already about six months behind. The previous year hadn't been finalized in the books, and the only things being done were monthly billings and supplier invoices.

Which were also sorely behind in payment.

So I buckled down, threatened to quit every day for two weeks, but finally pulled off their fiscal year end just two weeks late.

Not bad, considering there was only me in the department and given the sorry state of everything else. I found unpaid supplier invoices stashed in drawers and under files because the accountant couldn't deal with calls for payment. I discovered unbilled charges to clients in the hundreds of thousands of dollars because they didn't have a proper purchase order system in place.

In short, I pulled off a miracle.

But what I did was nothing compared to what God can do in us and through us. Of course, the biggest miracle is the gift of salvation. Another miracle is that He would even bother with us. Not to mention the changes in a redeemed life. And our desire to do what He did: love the unlovable and bring everyone into the Kingdom.

Today, as you consider the miracles God has worked in your life, miracles that we truly cannot understand or replicate, let's thank Him once more for Who He is.

Lord God Almighty, we look to You as the author and perfector of our faith. Thank you for the changes You have made in us, and help us to see others as You see them. In Jesus' name, Amen.

C0UNT1NG TH3 DAY$

My Journal

Day 19
Close Enough Isn't Good Enough

Genesis 18:28 "What if the number of the righteous is five less than fifty? Will you destroy the whole city because of five people?" "If I find forty-five there," He said, "I will not destroy it." (NIV)

Five less than fifty. Doesn't sound like a good reason to destroy a whole city, just because there are forty-five righteous people there instead of fifty. And God agrees; He will save the city for forty-five. We know that Abraham continues to bargain with God, until he gets God to agree that even if only ten righteous people can be found, God will spare the city.

Can you imagine the confusion that would be caused if we treated our financial projects that way? I was reminded of this one day when I was reconciling the bank accounts for the company I worked for. There was a difference of several thousand dollars. For some, that would be an 'acceptable' difference. For me, it was unthinkable that I would adjust for this amount. For me, reconciling the bank account means holding my records to the standard, the bank balance.

Isn't our spiritual life the same? We are taught to hold our lives accountable to the standard, Jesus. If I went around and determined whether my actions were 'close enough' to the standard, I suspect I would lower the standard. And when I next compared to the standard, Jesus, it would be a lesser Jesus than before.

God doesn't change, Jesus doesn't change—the only one who should be changing is me, to become more like them. 'Close enough' isn't close enough. I want to be like Him, so that someday I will know Him as I am known.

Lord, remind me that You are the only true standard to compare myself to. Your word says that everyone has missed the mark, and everyone deserves punishment. Thank You that Jesus has paid that price for me. Don't ever let me settle for 'close enough'. Amen.

C0UNT1NG TH3 DAY$

My Journal

Day 20
Lack and Need

Ecclesiastes 1:15 What is twisted cannot be straightened; what is lacking cannot be counted. (NIV)

Lack of money. Lack of time. Lack of leadership. Lack of capital. Lack of vision. Lack of resources. Lack of sales. Lack of staff. Lack of supply. Lack of—in business, we can go on and on about the reasons why companies fail.

In many cases, however, the problem doesn't lie in the exterior lacks, such as sales, staff, resources, or supply of products. Most often, the problem is within the personnel involved—training, vision, leadership. Integrity.

A company I once worked for had plenty of all the assets needed to run their optometrist/eyeglass business. The husband was the optometrist and his wife ran the business side, including the eyeglass sales and service.

They had competing visions. He wanted to get as many customers in and out of his office as possible, sending them out with new prescriptions so they would purchase eyeglasses. His wife was more focused on service than sales, so inevitably they didn't have enough selection, suppliers didn't get paid on time, and patients went elsewhere to buy their glasses because of long wait times as she gave personalized service to each customer.

Neither of them saw what was lacking in themselves. The husband needed to focus less on churning out prescriptions and more on making certain he did a good job at providing a good prescription. The wife needed to hire staff to help with customer service while she looked after the business end of things. Unfortunately, neither would listen to me and the company went out of business within a few years.

God offers us straight paths to follow, narrow to be sure but nonetheless plain to see. He also provides all we need, meaning we are never in lack when we are in God. Today, as you consider our verse, remind yourself that if we lack, there is a failing in us, not in God. Perhaps what we feel we need isn't needful at all.

Heavenly Father, thank You for reminding me that You are the God that owns the cattle on a thousand hills, and You own the hills as well. Anything I lack is not because of You. Make me grateful for what I have, and keep me humble enough to always need You. In Jesus' name, Amen.

C0UNT1NG TH3 DAY$

My Journal

Day 21
Count My Steps

Job 14:16 Surely then you will count my steps but not keep track of my sin. (NIV)

Job certainly had reason to turn to God in prayer, given all the calamities he experienced in his life. He'd lost his children, his wealth, and his health, and still God calls him righteous. I believe that's because God saw the end from the beginning, and He knew that Job repented of his attitude and his anger towards the God of the universe.

Many of us have been angry with God at least once in our lives, perhaps because of something we felt God should have done and didn't. Sometimes, however, our anger is aimed at God because of something we think He did that we feel He shouldn't have done. Usually this is because of an unexpected event in our lives.

I've been angry at God at least once. One time, I was going through a tough period when my cat died, my then-husband left me, and I lost my job at that advertising agency. I remember looking up to the heavens and saying, "Okay, God, what else are you going to take?" Most sensible people would stand aside to avoid the lightning bolt, but I didn't have even enough sense to do that. I felt that as a child of God, He should have taken better care of me.

But here's the thing: God was taking care of me. I was able to recover my health because I didn't have to deal with an abusive ex-husband who was draining the life from me. I didn't have to deal with a job that kept asking more and more and giving me less and less. I started a small accounting business from my home, had clients who were more like friends, worked the hours I wanted, recovered my health and my finances.

My anger at God didn't last long, because I saw how He was working in my life and making things better than I could have imagined. And He didn't hold my anger against me. You see, I have an advocate—Jesus—who stepped in and said, "Father, don't punish her. I know how she feels. See, I lost my family, my friends, lived under worse conditions, and I know she's going to come through this." Because of that covering, God saw Jesus and not me.

Today, as you think of the ways God doesn't hold your sin against you, thank Him for having only your good plans in His heart.

Lord, I worship You and thank You for all Your good plans for me. Give me patience as those good plans unfold, and open my eyes to see them. In Jesus' name, Amen.

C0UNT1NG TH3 DAY$

My Journal

Day 22
Increase Your Numbers

Genesis 17:2 "I will confirm my covenant between Me and you and will greatly increase your numbers." (NIV)

Ever had one of those days when you just didn't seem to get anything done? The to-do list gets longer, the in-box gets more full, the phone doesn't stop ringing. And just when you've had it up to here, the boss comes in with another project that needs to be done yesterday.

It's days like this that an increase in numbers doesn't sound so great. Or does it? If you could just double or triple your staff, you could get all this work done. If you could double or triple your vacation days, life would be easier. Or, if you could double your salary, the job would look a lot more attractive.

When God told Abram He would greatly increase his numbers because of His covenant with him, Abram didn't see the reality of that promise right away. In fact, he died not seeing the increase he was expecting. However, God credited him as a 'man of faith' because he stood on God's promise.

God wants to greatly increase your numbers, too. It may not come about as quickly as you want, or in the way you expect, but let's strive to be credited as a 'child of faith' because we stand on God's word.

Father, remind me that Your word is true, whether I see the outcome or not. Remind me that Your word is forever, whether it turns out the way I expect or not. Remind me that Your word is esteemed above all else. Amen.

C0UNT1NG TH3 DAY$

My Journal

Day 23
Balancing Act

Isaiah 46:5 "To whom will you compare me or count me equal? To whom will you liken me that we may be compared?" (NIV)

Balancing a checkbook is a system of comparing one set of numbers to another and making sure they are equal. With the onset of computerized banking, very seldom are the bank statements wrong. Unlike the old days when a brought forward balance could be mis-keyed from one statement to the next, computers tend to keep track of those numbers.

Most often, an un-reconciled account happens when someone puts in a wrong amount for a check or a deposit, fails to record an entry, or clears an entry incorrectly. I once had a problem with an account because I deleted a check that was marked as cleared, which resulted in my opening balance for the next month being different than on the previous reconciliation.

I spent about two days trying to find the difference, convinced that the bank had to be wrong.

But it wasn't. Once I found the entry, I resolved not to do that again!

When we reconcile an account, we must balance our numbers

to a proven standard, usually the bank accounts. But sometimes I have found myself comparing myself to something less than a proven standard. God is our creator, our proven standard. He never changes, is always steadfast, reliable, trustworthy. Those things I compare myself to which belong to this world will change—society's expectations, cultural norms, someone else's parameters, my own list.

An unproven standard is dangerous, because we might end up looking at a low standard, such as moral conduct, and thinking that we are at least better than that person. Or we might look at a picture of a fashion model and find ourselves sorely lacking.

No, God is our standard. Next to Him, we will find ourselves lacking. But because of the blood of Jesus, we know we are covered, that God doesn't see us but sees Jesus. This comparison encourages us onward and upward, willing to change more into the likeness of Jesus, so that when God looks at us, He sees more of Jesus and less of us.

Today, remind yourself that God is your standard. Your only standard.

God, forgive me for comparing myself to other people and other behaviors and other things. Thank You for making me worthy through the sacrifice of Your Son. In Jesus' name, Amen.

C0UNT1NG TH3 DAY$

My Journal

Day 24
Increased Output

II Thessalonians 1:11 . . . We constantly pray for you, that our God may count you worthy of His calling, and that by His power He may fulfill every good purpose of yours and every act prompted by your faith. (NIV)

One way to increase output is to add another input. For example, many orange juice producers add water to their juice to dilute the product and increase their output. Add bread crumbs to ground beef and you end up with more meatloaf. Add sugar to green peas and you end up with a tastier vegetable so you can use a cheaper, lower grade pea. Add more fat to your muffin mix and you end up with a greater number of muffins that make you feel full for a longer time.

We've talked about multiplication previously, but our verse today reminds us of another form of increase—through prayer. This verse tells us that prayers on our behalf intercede for us in the heavenlies and causes Him to turn everything we do to good.

Unlike adding bread crumbs or sugar or fat to our lives, God's increase has eternal consequences, builds our faith, and makes us more useful in His kingdom.

God's addition to our meager input multiplies our output beyond what we could think or imagine. He is not limited by us, but chooses to align Himself with us so that the world will see Him through us.

Today, consider how God has taken what you've committed to Him and made it bigger and better than you ever dreamed.

Lord God, thank You for using me for Your purposes, for making up for my shortcomings, for allowing me to participate in Your marvelous plans. In Jesus' name, Amen.

C0UNT1NG TH3 DAY$

My Journal

Day 25
Numbers without Number

Psalm 139:18 Were I to count them, they would outnumber the grains of sand. When I awake, I am still with You. (NIV)

When I think about the national debt, the number astounds me: 18.2 trillion dollars. If you were to lay 18.2 trillion one-dollar bills end to end, they would encircle the earth nearly 70,000 times. If you stacked them vertically, they would reach over 1.2 million miles in height. That's about the distance from Earth to the moon five times. If you were to count them out in one-dollar increments at the rate of 2 per second, it would take you nearly 300,000 years. If you were to divide them amongst every citizen in the US today, we would each owe almost fifty-seven thousand dollars.

Those are phenomenal numbers.

And yet, those numbers are a mere fraction of the number of thoughts God has about us. The psalmist says that the number of His thoughts outnumber the grains of sand in the world.

The psalmist acknowledges the phenomenal size of a God Who can know this number. And yet, this God is also personal to each of us. He hears our prayers, knows our needs, answers our calls, catches our tears in a jar, and still has compassion and patience to draw us to Himself, bring us to salvation, change us into His likeness and image, and call us His own.

Today, consider the majesty and humility of a God who knows He is better than us, yet doesn't constantly rub that holiness into our faces, instead choosing to anoint us with His righteousness and direct us in His path.

Righteous and holy God, I thank You for treating me with more love and patience than I deserve. Show me how to extend that love and patience to others You put in my path today. In Jesus' name, Amen.

C0UNT1NG TH3 DAY$

My Journal

Day 26

Boundaries

Deuteronomy 32:8 When the Most High gave the nations their inheritance, when He divided all mankind, He set up boundaries for the peoples according to the number of the sons of Israel. (NIV)

Ten-column paper. Twenty-four-column paper. Call me old school. I don't care. I love those columnar pads. Started my first bookkeeping business using them. My first three clients were handwritten in those sheets.

I liked those green pages with all the lines and columns because I had to write neat to keep my descriptions and numbers inside the little tiny spaces allowed.

Boundaries. A good thing to know. That's the cool thing about the Bible. It's like a columnar pad that shows you how far you can go. Don't write outside the lines. Don't step over this line in the sand. God always tells you what is good for you and what isn't.

Setting up boundaries wasn't in His original plan. He gave Adam and Eve the run of the garden, but because of their sin, they were shown out the door.

However, He set up an angel with a flaming sword to show us the way back TO the garden.

Just like the horizontal and vertical lines on the columnar pad show us where to put our numbers, God's word shows us how to thrive and prosper in the world He created.

Today, pull out one of those pads and try balancing your check book or write in your household expenses for the month. Not so easy, is it?

God, thank You for setting boundaries for us, so we know where to go and how to follow You. We praise You that You are a God who wants good for us. In Jesus' name, Amen.

C0UNT1NG TH3 DAY$

My Journal

Day 27

Count Your Blessings

Romans 4:8 Blessed is the man whose sin the Lord will never count against him. (NIV)

We learn to count at a very young age. One number at a time, getting bigger and bigger, until we don't think we can get any bigger, and then we add just one more. Then another. Then another. Until we finally understand that there is no end to the numbers we can count.

Numbers are like that, always increasing to amazing proportions, always one more.

Just like God. As we grow in Him, we increase in our understanding of Him. Just when we think we know Him, He amazes us with just one more revelation, one more miracle, one more gift that we know we don't deserve.

When God calls us into His kingdom, He makes us a promise: He will cast our sin as far as the east is from the west, into the sea of forgetfulness. What a promise. As financial folk, we tend to keep track of things like money, inventory, labor hours, assets, debt.

And yet the biggest debt in the world—our sin—paid by the

biggest giver in the world—Jesus—and forgiven by the biggest asset-holder in the world—God—has been cast aside as though it were trash.

Which, of course, it is.

There is no room in the kingdom of God for sin. There is no sin in heaven. And we must strive to have no sin in our lives, either.

Today, when the enemy tries to remind you of your past, respond the same way God does: what sin?

Gracious Father, thank You that You have forgiven me, that you don't remember my sin or throw it in my face. Give me strength to rebuke the enemy today. In Jesus' name. Amen.

C0UNT1NG TH3 DAY$

My Journal

Day 28
Reconciling Accounts

2 Corinthians 5:19 . . . God was reconciling the world to himself in Christ, not counting men's sins against them. And He has committed to us the message of reconciliation. (NIV)

Reconciling bank accounts and ledgers on a monthly basis used to be a regular part of my job when I worked in a bank. In those days, we stored our ledgers on cards in trays that we wheeled in and out of the vault every day, because those ledgers were like money. If we lost one, we had no record of what money a customer held in our bank or what debt they owed.

We manually listed every card each month to make sure the total agreed with the total held on the books of the bank for every account, every loan, every investment. Using one of those old-fashioned adding machines with the punch buttons, the tape, and the pull handle for when the power went out, we had to account for every card.

Problems happened when we failed to make sure we had no total in the machine before we started listing the cards. For example, if someone had used the machine previously and simply totaled their numbers, and then we came along and began adding in our cards, the machine picked up the previous total and continued. Even if we printed a tape of the numbers we punched in, the total wouldn't be right because of the carried-forward total which we couldn't see because it wasn't printed on the tape.

I learned this the hard way, and made it a point to hit Total twice until 0.00 showed at the beginning of my tape, because trying to balance when you can't see the input was impossible. All the cards checked off, but the numbers were still wrong otherwise.

What a joy to serve a God who has reconciled us to Himself. He is the perfect balance, the one we want to be like, to agree with, to be worthy of the price paid by Jesus.

Today, commit to God that you will not allow outside influences to distract you from His perfect plan for you.

Lord, thank You for reconciling me to You. I know that's the best and safest place to be. In Jesus' name, Amen.

C0UNT1NG TH3 DAY$

My Journal

Day 29

If We Just Had More

Genesis 26:24 That night the LORD appeared to him and said, "I am the God of your father Abraham. Do not be afraid, for I am with you; I will bless you and will increase the number of your descendants for the sake of my servant Abraham." (NIV)

Many of us live our lives thinking that if we just made more money, if we just had a bigger house, a newer car, whatever that 'more' is that we want, we would be happy. But the truth is—and we know this deep inside our heart—that if we had that one thing more, we still wouldn't be satisfied.

God wants us to learn the principles of Contentment Living. As the Apostle Paul said, he's been rich and he's been poor, and he's learned to live with what he has. "I have learned to be content whatever the circumstances." Phil 4:11 (NIV)

When we focus on the Kingdom of God instead of our own kingdom, we are reminded we won't lack for anything. All of our needs are provided for, and we have plenty left over to share with others. Healing is ours, the righteous never are homeless or go begging bread.

God is our Jehovah Jireh, our provider. And He isn't talking only about the sweet by and by—no, He has placed us in a world that requires food, clothing, housing, and, in most societies, some sort of currency. Our problem is we often forget that it is the work of God's hands, not ours, that provides the increase.

Today, let's focus on God and who He is, rather than on what He will give us. Let's remember that He is the one who owns the cattle on a thousand hills, and he owns the hills, too.

Heavenly Father, my Jehovah Jireh, please keep me mindful of who You are, not only on what You do for me. Truthfully, if You gave me nothing except my salvation, I would have all that I need. But I want a deeper relationship with You, so please, Lord, draw me closer to you today. In Jesus' name, Amen.

C0UNT1NG TH3 DAY$

My Journal

Day 30
God of All

Genesis 8:17 Bring out every kind of living creature that is with you—the birds, the animals, and all the creatures that move along the ground—so they can multiply on the earth and be fruitful and increase in number upon it. (NIV)

God loves multiplication.

He says a number of times in His word that we are to go forth and multiply, that all of His creation is to multiply and fill the earth.

Why would He want that? Why didn't He simply make the earth smaller so we didn't need all this multiplication?

Because He wants to show us the bigger picture of who He is. If there were only a handful of people and a few animals, we wouldn't realize how powerful He is.

If there was only one kind of dog, we wouldn't see how creative He is.

If there was only one kind of flower, we wouldn't understand how much He loves beauty.

And if there was only one kind of people, we wouldn't see the true picture of who God is, because we are made in His likeness and image.

So, all of this variety is for our benefit.

Today as you think on this, ask God to grow in you a love for His diversity and His mathematics.

God of all, show Yourself to me in the variety around me. From the different kinds of birds to the different fishes in the sea to the intricacy of plants and insects, help me see beauty in all You have created. In Jesus' name, Amen.

C0UNT1NG TH3 DAY$

My Journal

Day 31
Complete Honesty

II Kings 12:15 They did not require an accounting from those to whom they gave the money to pay the workers, because they acted with complete honesty. (NIV)

Money will buy many things in this world, but there are things no amount of dollars will purchase: peace of mind, sweet sleep, and a good reputation are but some.

In our scripture verse today, the men put in charge of collecting the offerings were not required to give an accounting. In other words, they didn't have to keep records. All they had to do was empty the chest when it got full and put an empty one in its place to collect the offerings.

The reason they were so trusted was because they acted with complete honesty. But let's get this straight: their honesty didn't begin with this assignment.

Their honesty was complete. It infiltrated every aspect of their lives. They didn't just have a good reputation for being honest men; they had an impeccable reputation. Nobody could bring a charge against them. Nobody could whisper that there was any kind of shenanigans going on with their business dealings. No nasty rumors. They were squeaky clean.

Some day we will stand before God, and He will judge our lives. Our sin is covered by the blood of Christ, so in that respect, we will be squeaky clean.

But what about those areas of our lives that nobody except God will see? Do we treat others fairly? Do we strive to put in a good day's work? Do we take the hard path and not cut corners to save a few minutes or a few dollars? Could we be described as "completely honest"?

Today, as we finish our thirty-one days of devotions and look forward to the future, let's commit to being completely honest in everything we do: in our work, in our family life, in our relationships with others, and most of all, with God.

Heavenly Father, thank You for this journey of faith and relationship we've traveled this past month. Help me to remember those precepts You have placed in my heart, as together we walk forward in complete honesty. In Jesus' name, Amen.

C0UNT1NG TH3 DAY$

My Journal

Made in the USA
Monee, IL
22 October 2020